Wimbledon
Then and Now

Pictures from Old Postcards
contrasted with
Present - day Photographs

by
Richard Milward

Photographs by
Roger Musgrave and Angela Rathbone

S. B. Publications

D0774645

To the Wimbledon Society
which has done so much
to preserve all that is of value
in this area

First published in 1995 by S.B. Publications
c/o 19 Grove Road, Seaford, East Sussex BN25 1TP

ISBN 1 85770 089 9

Typeset and Printed by Island Press Ltd.
3 Cradle Hill Industrial Estate, Seaford, East Sussex BN25 3JE

CONTENTS

ACKNOWLEDGMENTS

To Lady Hartopp and the Museum Committee of the Wimbledon Society for permission to make use of their collection of old postcards for many of the 'Then' pictures in this book.

To Keith Every for allowing me to use eight 'Then' pictures (numbers 11,12,17,26,35,37,42,43) from his wonderful postcard collection.

To Roger Musgrave for his care, patience and expertise in taking the great majority of the 'Now' photographs.

To Angela Rathbone for readily agreeing to take extra 'Now' pictures at short notice and producing eight excellent views (numbers 11,12,17,26,35,37,42,43).

To Paul Bowness for his help in getting all the pictures processed and to Les Kirkin for carrying out the work, especially the enhancing of several old photos which originally were barely visible.

And to Anne-Marie Hill for her kindness in typing the manuscript so quickly and expertly.

BIBLIOGRAPHY

Milward, R.J. : *Historic Wimbledon* (1989).

Wimbledon : A Pictorial History (1994).

Plastow, N. : *Safe as houses : Wimbledon, 1939-45* (1990).

A History of Wimbledon and Putney Commons (1988).

A Guide to Wimbledon, 1907.

Kelly's Directory of Wimbledon, 1912-13.

HISTORICAL INTRODUCTION

Wimbledon's long and distinguished history has been shaped by four main factors: its hill, its leading residents, its railway and its local government.

Its hill provided early settlers with important advantages. Beyond its edge lay a large plateau (the site of the future Common) which assured them of a good water supply, good grazing for their animals and a good view over the surrounding country. Hence it was chosen as the site first of a Bronze Age hill-fort (later wrongly named Caesar's Camp) and then of a Saxon settlement, perhaps founded by a leader called Wynnman. By the early thirteenth century a village known as 'Wimeldon' formed part of one of the many estates of the Archbishops of Canterbury. During the next century it was seriously affected by outbreaks of plague, yet by the reign of Henry VIII it was producing good crops of corn, hay, fruit and vegetables, as well as timber, wool, cheese and even wine.

Nonetheless Wimbledon remained small and isolated until a leading member of Edward VI's Council, Sir William Cecil, decided to lease the one large brick mansion, the Rectory, as a country retreat. His example led his eldest son, Thomas, Earl of Exeter, to build a magnificent Elizabethan manor house on the slope of the hill to the east of the Rectory. There he entertained the old Queen in the 1590s and later King James I. As a result, he helped to transform the village into a summer home for wealthy gentlemen,who built large mansions in the High Street (notably Eagle House, erected about 1613 by a rich merchant, Robert Bell) and around the Common. Important families like the Spencers, the Marryats and the Pepys came to live here and to run large estates which brought the area considerable prestige, as well as providing work for local tradesmen and farmers, such as the Masons and the Watneys.

At the start of Queen Victoria's reign Wimbledon could still be described as 'a beautiful and highly genteel village'. Sixty years later, however, it had become a major suburb of London, thanks to the opening of the London and South-Western Railway in 1838, the laying-on of a supply of mains water from 1850 and the availability of relatively cheap land. New roads were laid out and rows of small terraced houses built south of the railway in 'New Wimbledon'. Large, architect-designed mansions standing in spacious grounds went up in Wimbledon Park and along Copse Hill. Life in the new suburb produced many social problems: poorly built houses, inadequate schools, infectious diseases, unemployment and 'the demon drink'. Churchmen, both Anglican and Nonconformist, did a lot to make conditions more bearable, but it was only the efforts of new local authorities, starting with a Local

Board of Health in 1866, that helped to control disease and make the new suburb 'a desirable place of residence'.

For another century Wimbledon continued to govern itself, from 1905 as a Borough with its own coat of arms. In 1965, however, it was merged with the Urban District of Merton and Morden, and the Borough of Mitcham in the new London Borough of Merton. This so-called 'shot-gun marriage' was far from popular and has led to a lot of controversial changes, above all the removal of the new Council's headquarters to Morden and the development of the old Town Hall as a shopping-centre. Yet Wimbledon has kept its individual character, helped by its incomparable Common (saved from enclosure as a park in 1871), its genuine sense of community (shown by the influence of the Wimbledon Society and the many residents' associations) and its world-wide fame from the Lawn Tennis Championships which started in 1877.

Such a history is proof of the saying that 'every age is an age of change'. Medieval peasants, Tudor farmers, Georgian craftsmen and Victorian railway-workers all discussed and probably resented the changes they saw taking place round them. But in the twentieth century, above all in the past thirty years, change has been on a far greater scale and has come at a pace unknown in any previous age. Many Wimbledonians have been left bewildered and even horrified by the transformation of the town centre, the disappearance of small family shops, the unending procession of cars and huge lorries, and the threat to their hospitals and open spaces. Yet amid all the undoubted changes Wimbledon has kept far more links with its past than have its neighbours, Kingston and Croydon.

Change and continuity are the twin themes of the series of photographs reproduced in this book. They are arranged in the form of a tour of Wimbledon, starting at the Windmill, going south through the village and town centre to the old boundary with Merton, before diverting east to Wimbledon Park and west to Cottenham Park. The 'Then' pictures are mainly taken from postcards printed between 1900 and 1914. Opposite each appear the same views taken in the spring and early summer of 1995. In some cases the view-point has had to be slightly changed either because of danger to the life of the photographer or because new trees block the old picture. Otherwise it is hoped that the comparison of 'Then' and 'Now' will give readers some idea of what they have lost - and gained - by living in Wimbledon in the 1990s rather than in the 1900s.

Richard Milward.
June 1995.

4798, THE WINDMILL, WIMBLEDON COMMON

THE WINDMILL

The Windmill about 1920. Built a hundred years earlier, it had long ceased to be a working mill, and was now divided into three small cottages. Described in the Borough guide-book as 'the most conspicuous feature on the Common', it could still be seen from Southside and had become a focus for walkers, picnic parties and motor cyclists, but hardly yet for many cars.

The Windmill 1995. Now a museum, it attracts thousands of visitors a year, hence the café in front. The huge car park which can take 300 cars is often full, as on this Sunday in June. But with many more trees and bushes on the Common than seventy years ago, the Windmill can be seen better from Richmond Park than from Parkside.

CAESAR'S WELL

Then: Caesar's Well about 1905. A natural spring, it has no known connection with any Roman. In 1872 it was surrounded by large granite blocks and a ring of fir trees, placed there by 'H.W.P.' (Sir Henry Peek M.P.) to commemorate the passing of the Commons Act the previous year. It was a favourite spot for Edwardian picnics.

Now: The Well today, with the granite blocks looking the worse for wear. At least two of the old fir trees survive, while in the background is thick vegetation. The water, however, now comes from a stand-pipe which taps the spring from eighteen feet down.

WEST PLACE

Then: West Place about 1905, built on land enclosed from the Common in the eighteenth century. In the foreground by the carriage is Dormer's 'Livery and Bait Stables, Broughams and Carriages (for hire)'. Next door is the tall, ivy clad Hermitage and a row of small cottages, which cost about £100 each to build. Behind them is the Beulah Laundry and beyond are the large houses of North View, with the edge of a very open Common to the right.

Now: West Place in 1995. Dormer's has become an antiques shop. The laundry has gone, while the cottages are now in demand as retirement homes and, thoroughly modernised, sell for up to £300,000. The road is ideal parking space for a walk on the overgrown Common or a visit to the Fox and Grapes round the corner in Camp Road.

PARKSIDE AND THE POUND.
Then: Parkside and the Pound about 1905 (from a tinted postcard). Horse buses are travelling to and from Putney. To the right are the outlines of large houses recently built on the old Wimbledon House estate. On the left the Pound is still occasionally used to keep horses and cows which stray when grazing on the Common. In the centre are some young trees recently planted by the Conservators and a drinking fountain, 'the gift of Robert Hanbury Esq M.P.', a Tory Cabinet minister who died in 1903.

Now: Parkside and the Pound in 1995. The road is now far busier, the vegetation far thicker. But the Pound survives as a link with the past. In the second world war a camouflaged pillbox was built inside it. At least two of the trees planted ninety years ago seem to have survived.

Rushmere Pond, The Common, Wimbledon.

RUSHMERE POND.
Then: Rushmere Pond about 1930, popular with children for paddling and sailing their boats. During severe winters in the 1930s it froze sufficiently to allow skating on the ice. In the background is the Green with white houses which date from the late eighteenth century. On the right is Southside with the gable of a house clearly visible over the trees. And not a car is in sight.

Now: Rushmere today, with cars parked nose to tail in front of the Green. The sky-line has also been altered, especially by the pyramid roof of the office block on the left. During recent dry summers the pond noticeably shrank, but now it is as full as in the 1930s – and as good for a paddle.

SOUTHSIDE

Then: Southside about 1905, with the beeches on the edge of the Common just growing up, while the elms on the other side of the road probably date from 1760 when Southside was first laid out. On the left of the picture are the railings in front of Wimbledon Lodge, soon to be pulled down and Murray Road developed. In the background is Westside.

Now: Southside in 1995. The beeches have grown up, while the old elms have been cut down. The road is now a car park for the village, but horse-riders have their own track at its side.

CROOKED BILLET.
Then: The Crooked Billet about 1950, a collection of old cottages (some dating back to the seventeenth century) with two not very fashionable pubs on the right (one giving its name to the area) and three small shops in the right foreground. The Cinque cottages (in the background behind the inn sign) had been built in 1872 by Sir Henry Peek M.P. for 'poor men of good character in needy circumstances'.

Now: The Crooked Billet today, a far more fashionable area. Its buildings including the Cinque cottages have been renovated and the shops have been turned back into cottages. The green outside the two pubs, the Crooked Billet and the Hand-in-Hand, is now the scene for large drinking parties, especially at week-ends.

SOUTHSIDE HOUSE.

Then: Southside House, Woodhayes Road, in 1903, then two houses as it had been ever since 1751, when it had been described as 'not quite finished'. The half to the left (unnamed) is only notable as the house of the Wright family (1804-45), after whom the alley to the Ridgway is named. The other half (known as Holme Lodge) was leased from 1801 to 1812 by the Lockes. Charles Locke, British Consul-General at Naples in the 1790s, had been a bitter enemy of Emma Hamilton.

Now: Southside House in 1995, now almost lost in vegetation which has flourished in the past eighty years. The two houses were converted into a single large and imposing mansion in the 1930s by Mrs. Munthe, widow of the novelist Axel Munthe. Their son Malcolm has recently made the house a great tourist attraction with its new cupola, its fine rooms and its exceptional art collection.

HAMPTON'S

Then: Hampton and Sons first office at the top of the High Street about 1910. The London estate agents had recently begun to develop the Wimbledon House estate on Parkside. The old mansion had been pulled down in 1900, Marryat Road (named after a nineteenth century owner) laid out on its site and large architect-designed houses built in its grounds. Opposite the office is the garden of one of the new houses on the Green. Beyond is the High Street with a motor car and a delivery van.

Now: Hampton's office 1995, by the end of Marryat Road. Behind it the belt of old trees has been replaced with a block of new offices. As a result the Rose and Crown, a seventeenth century inn, is far more visible.

4795 HIGH STREET. WIMBLEDON

THE HIGH STREET FROM THE ROSE AND CROWN

Then: The High Street looking south from near the Rose and Crown about 1920. Two London buses and a few cars provide the modern note. Otherwise the shops on the right are nearly all Georgian, while the railings and trees on the left stand in front of the Jacobean Eagle House. In the background is the Dog and Fox, a very old inn, rebuilt in the 1870s.

Now: The High Street in 1995 with its stream of cars, buses, fire-engine, taxi – and obtrusive lights.
Yet many of the Georgian shops, as well as Eagle House, survive.

THE HIGH STREET FROM THE DOG AND FOX.
Then: The High Street looking north from in front of the Dog and Fox about 1924. The small shops on the right date from the 1830s. Among them is Frost's, a post office and stationers, where the poet Swinburne used to call after his daily visit to the Rose and Crown. Opposite is the entrance to Allington Close, then known as Bee Hive Buildings. In the background is the large turreted shop of Thomas Mason 'grocer and postmaster', a business which started about 1800.

Now: The High Street today. The old shops on the right are still there, though the goods they sell are now very different. Those in the foreground opposite have also survived after facelifts. But Masons has long gone and been replaced by a large modern building which hardly seems in keeping with the rest of the village.

WIMBLEDON. — HIGH STREET AND FIRE STATION.

HIGH STREET AND FIRE STATION

Then: The High Street at the junction with Church Road about 1905. To the right is the large Fire Station built in 1890 to house a new 'steamer', christened 'May Queen'. The horses were stabled to the rear of the Dog and Fox to the left. At the side of the Station is a small Ale House, the Brewery Tap, once known as the Lord Palmerston. In the road the Putney bus is collecting passengers on a warm sunny day, shown by the number of ladies on the open top deck.

Now: The junction with Church Road today. The fire engine was moved to Queens Road in 1907 and the Station converted into shops. More recently the old bell was returned to the turret and a Civic Trust plaque placed below the round window to mark the Village Improvement Scheme of 1967. The Brewery Tap has clearly been enlarged, taking over the 'fruiterers' of 1905.

THE SOUTHERN END OF THE HIGH STREET

Then: The southern end of the High Street at the junction with the Ridgway and Wimbledon Hill about 1910. The magnificent London and County Bank building and the shops beyond it have just been built on land once part of the old Belvedere estate. In front of them are the Toynbee Fountain and a horses' drinking trough. Standen's Bakery on the left is the oldest shop in this part of the High Street and dates from the late 1850s.

Now: The southern High Street in 1995, with the buildings substantially unchanged. But apart from the bank (now the Nat-West) and the bakery (now Gravestock's), their use has greatly altered, with an estate agent and a wine shop prominent on the left. The even more prominent 'street furniture' shows the extent to which the car now dominates the area.

THE RIDGWAY

Then: The Ridgway shopping parade about 1910. On the left are a greengrocer's, a 'house decorator' and Norman Jenkins, stationer and publisher of this postcard. On the other side of Denmark Road are Arthur Cocke, grocer and post office, a baker and a butcher. Beyond the shops are two public houses, the King of Denmark and the Swan, with stables next door. All were built about 1860 to serve the houses going up to the south of the Ridgway. The big pole in front of the King of Denmark is for the new telephone.

Now: The Ridgway today. The decorator's and stationer's survive under different management, as do the pubs. But the shops in Denmark Terrace have completely changed and the clock over the grocer's has sadly vanished. The telephone pole has been succeeded by even more unsightly street lights.

WIMBLEDON HILL

Then: The bottom of Wimbledon Hill about 1905. 'Few towns', the Borough guide-book claimed, 'can boast of as charming an approach'. The land on the right with the path and the line of beautiful trees had not long been taken over from the Belvedere estate. But an old 'finger post' had been left pointing along Woodside to Summerstown, Garratt and Wandsworth. The men standing at the edge of the road just above it are by the spot where Jack the trace-horse was to be kept between 1908 and 1939.

Now: The Hill in 1995, with fewer trees and far more traffic. To the left at the corner of Mansel Road is Wimbledon High School for Girls. Above it is the latest in the large blocks of flats that now line the Hill.

Hill Road,   Wimbledon

HILL ROAD.
Then: Hill Road from the junction with Mansel Road (to the right) and Woodside (to the left), about 1905. Below Woodside is Thomson's Nursery with its large conservatory and trees lining the pathway. Below Mansel Road, the shops (which date from the 1880s) include Cullen's (a grocer), Bowden's (a chemist), Randall's (boot-maker's), Southdown Farm Dairies and Wright Brothers, 'general draper's and court milliner's', with the large shop window.

Now: Hill Road today. Thomson's Nursery has long gone, as have the trees, while the shops just below Mansel Road have recently been replaced by an unimpressive modern block. But Wright's shop-front has somehow survived.

ELY'S CORNER

Then: Ely's Corner at the junction of Hill and Worple Roads about 1910. Joseph Ely had founded his draper's business near the station in 1876 and moved to this corner ten years later. The front of the shop with its crowded windows was rebuilt with a more gentle curve after the coming of the trams in 1907. On the opposite corner of Worple Road was the office of London United Tramways, whose 'speedy and well-appointed cars' were said to run at intervals of about two minutes and at very low fares.

Now: Ely's Corner 1995. The department store, after yet another rebuilding, still flourishes, while every building below it has changed. For once the modern street lights are not as obtrusive as the Edwardian lamp-posts and tram-line poles.

HILL ROAD NEAR THE STATION

Then: Hill Road near Wimbledon Station about 1910. A collection of small shops (dating from the 1870s and 1880s) is only notable for George Ely 'provision merchant' on the right, with Joseph Ely's original shop at the corner of Alexandra Road beyond it. In the background the trees on the pavement beyond the Public Library have disappeared.

Now: Hill Road in the summer of 1995. All the small shops have been swept away, those on the left in the 1980's by the St. George's development, those on the right in 1995 so as to widen the junction with Alexandra Road. The one link with the past are the Bank Buildings in the background.

THE STATION FORECOURT.

Then: The forecourt of the London and South-Western Railway Station about 1905. Drivers of the horse-drawn taxis, known as 'flys', stand waiting for fares. Behind them is the entrance to a bridge leading to the platforms and beyond that is the booking office. In the background is the District Line Station (opened in 1889) with its own 'flys'. In the centre a dog is begging, while the sky-line is dominated by high telephone posts and signal gantries.

Now: The forecourt of the station today, with the modern brand of 'horseless carriages'. The station building, which combines both Southern Region and District Railways, dates from 1930. The shops on the right were added a little later.

THE RAILWAY HOTEL

Then: The South-Western Hotel, photographed in the early 1980s not long before it was demolished. It first appears on a map of 1865 as the Mansel Tavern, named after the family that sold the land for the railway. By 1900 it had become the South-Western Hotel, after the London and South-Western Railway whose first station had been built just below. On the left are the first shops on the bridge, including the Estate Agents Hawes, in Wimbledon since the 1880s. On the right is one of the original Mansel Villas, built in the 1870s.

Now: By 1995 the Hotel and the shops have vanished. Its place has been taken by the end of the large St. George's office block and in particular by Dixon's shop. Commuters now have new pubs to serve them just up Hill Road. Their one link with the past is the pavement and its curb-stone

THE RAILWAY BRIDGE.

Then: Wimbledon Railway Bridge without any shops about 1910. Originally a small iron structure carrying the Merton Road over a Twin-track railway in 1838, it was now considerably wider and longer, and carried much more traffic. In this photo a tram going towards the Broadway has just passed a 'fly' cab going into the Station, a young cyclist pedalling dangerously between the tram tracks and to the right a private carriage on the wrong side of the road. The background is dominated by the massive Prince of Wales pub, already over thirty years old.

Now: The Bridge today. The first shops, put up in early 1930s, survive on the left. Opposite, however, they have been replaced by the controversial 'Fridge on the Bridge' with larger shops, including Smith's and Waterstone's. The bridge acts as a funnel for the cars, buses and lorries which pour north and south through Wimbledon. Behind it the Prince of Wales has recently been given a welcome face-lift and its clock again tells the time.

49

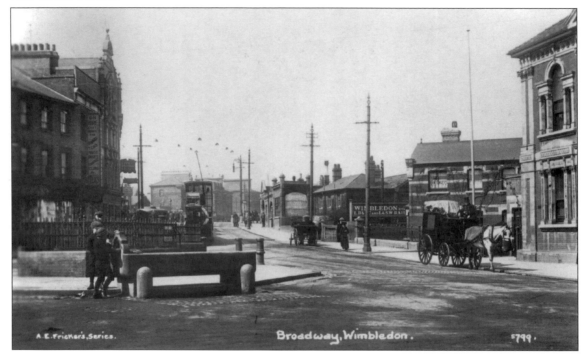

A.E.Fricker's Series.   Broadway, Wimbledon.   5799.

THE BROADWAY.

Then: The original Broadway, the broad expanse of road between the shops on the left and the first Town Hall on the right, photographed about 1910. Public lavatories were then provided for shoppers, as well as a drinking trough for horses and dogs (and a fountain for children). The back entrance to the station for both railway lines – the London, Brighton and South Coast, and London and South Western – is to the left of the Municipal Offices.

Now: The top of the Broadway today. The shops on the left survive. Opposite, two major changes have occurred: in the early 1930s a second Town Hall was opened on the site of the first and shops were built on the bridge; sixty years later this Town Hall was transformed into the Centre Court shopping complex, while the public lavatories were removed.

THE TOWN HALL

Then: Wimbledon's second Town Hall, about 1935. Dismissed by one authority as 'stone-faced, symmetrical and dull', the building at least looked like a genuine civic centre. It was opened by Prince George, later Duke of Kent, in 1931 and for over fifty years provided a dignified setting for grand occasions, regular meetings of the Council and day-to-day administration. In 1988 it was also the focus for wild celebrations when Wimbledon Football Club came home from Wembley with the F.A. Cup

Now: The ex-Town Hall today, now part of the Centre Court shopping complex. The facade has been retained, but the interior has been transformed. To its left an imposing rotunda now leads to the main shops built on the site of the old civic hall (which has yet to be replaced).

THE BROADWAY BY THE THEATRE.

Then: A picture of 'Xmas at Wimbledon, 1907' along the gaily decorated Broadway, then still known as Merton Road. The shops had been built twenty years or so earlier on land which for centuries had been part of Cowdrey Farm. They included a piano shop (on the corner of Kings Road), Lefevre's 'ladies outfitter' (the second with the awning down) and beyond them Thresher and Co 'wine and spirit merchants' and Freeman, Hardy and Willis 'boot and shoe makers'. Opposite on the right is the turning into Russell Road with stone setts to provide a clean crossing over the road.

Now: The Broadway today. Many of the old buildings survive behind their modern fronts, despite bombs falling all along this stretch of the road during the Blitz. On the right is the side of Wimbledon Theatre, opened three years after the earlier picture was taken.

MERTON ROAD BY ST. WINEFRIDE'S.
Then: Merton Road between Latimer and Ridley Roads about 1905. An early car turns the corner in front of the recently opened Roman Catholic church, St. Winefride's. On the right are shops built only a few years earlier in what had once been a corn field. Opposite behind the trees is the Wimbledon and Merton Liberal and Radical Club.

Now: Merton Road in 1995. The church and almost all the original buildings survive. Few bombs dropped in this part of South Wimbledon during the Second World War.

THE CROSS-ROADS, SOUTH WIMBLEDON.

Then: The cross-roads, South Wimbledon, the site of double turn-pike gates removed only forty years before this photograph was taken in about 1910. A tram going to Summerstown is turning from Merton Road on the left into Merton High Street. In the foreground a solitary cyclist stops at the end of Kingston Road, with the Grove Tavern on his right and the Grove Fish Bar behind the constable on point-duty.

Now: The cross-roads today, normally one of the busiest in the area. The Tavern has been rebuilt, but the shops on the left have survived. In the background on the right, South Wimbledon Underground Station, opened in 1926, has replaced the Fish Bar.

KINGSTON ROAD
Then: Kingston Road about 1910. The shops on the right (built twenty years earlier in the grounds of Holme Elms, a large eighteenth century mansion) are in Wimbledon, between the ends of Russell and Gladstone Roads. Dark jars outside two upstairs windows advertise an 'oilman's' business. In the background are trees beyond the level-crossing on the railway line to West Croydon.

Now: Kingston Road today. Most of the Wimbledon buildings survive, unlike those on the left in Merton. But whether this is to their advantage is another matter.

MERTON HIGH STREET AND THE WANDLE

Then: Merton High Street and the Wandle about 1905. The buildings on the right are in Wimbledon. The King's Head, one of the oldest public houses in the area, claims to have been founded in the reign of Henry VII. With its fine bow windows, it certainly goes back to Georgian times and was an important coaching inn.

Now: Merton High Street and the Wandle in 1995. Little survives from 1905 except perhaps the shops to the left of the pub – and the river. The King's Head was rebuilt in Young's Brewery style in 1931 and sited further from the road. Merton Bus Garage was built at its side in 1913.

HAYDONS ROAD.

Then: Haydons Road between Cromwell and Gap Roads about 1910. The tram to Summerstown is passing a long parade of small, new shops. The one on the right is a dairy. Opposite is a stationer, greengrocer, tobacconist, cheesemonger and builder. Cromwell House to the left of the tram is the home of Dr. Bickford, 'physician and surgeon'. The road is named after George Haydon who ran a local farm in the 1770s.

Now: Haydons Road today. The trams have gone, but most of the shops have survived, though now accompanied by unsightly advertisements and graffiti. The Doctor's surgery was bombed in the war and has been replaced by a petrol station.

WIMBLEDON. — WOODSIDE.

WOODSIDE.

Then: Woodside at the junction with St. Mary's and Lake Roads about 1905. The land on the left with its thick belt of trees was the southern edge of the old Wimbledon Park Estate. Its development started in the 1870s with the laying out of Lake Road and the erection of the ornamental brick pillars in the middle of the picture. On the far left the wall with the letterbox marks the boundary of **Queen Alexandra's Court** (The Royal Homes for the Widows and Unmarried Daughters of Army and Navy Officers), which had recently been opened by the King and Queen.

Now: Woodside 1995, with fewer trees to hide the post-war development of Lake Road, but with the brick pillars still in place. Queen Alexandra's Court is just visible on the left. The increase in traffic is evident from the width-regulators behind the car in the foreground.

Wimbledon. - Parish Church & Arthur Road in Winter

STAG LODGE AND ST. MARY'S

Then: Stag Lodge and St. Mary's Parish Church after a heavy snow-fall in the winter of 1882. The Lodge, built about 1850 as a gate-house for Wimbledon Park House, now supports boards advertising plots of land for sale along the newly laid-out Arthur Road. The reason for placing a stone stag on the front has never been discovered. The parish church with its famous spire had been rebuilt by Gilbert Scott in 1843. Its vicar was now Canon Haygarth.

Now: Stag Lodge and the Parish Church today. The fine new stag was put up in 1988 after the original one had accidentally been smashed at the start of the Second World War. St. Mary's recently celebrated the 150th anniversary of its rebuilding. Arthur Road, however, has been transformed into a major traffic route to London.

DAIRY WALK.
Then: Dairy Walk about 1900. This narrow path through the wooded edge of Wimbledon Park estate linked a Dairy Farm established by Earl Spencer to Church Road and so to St Mary's. The interest of this picture lies in the fact that it only covered half the postcard. Not until 1902 did the Post Office allow the message to go with the address on the front, leaving the other full side for the picture. From this change dated the amazing popularity of postcards with over 800 million being sent every year until 1914.

Now: Dairy Walk in 1995, as it now emerges into Marryat Road. It has barely survived as a faded relic from the past amid a rash of modern development and official notices.

THE END OF MARRYAT ROAD.
Then: The end of Marryat Road about 1910. Building on the old Wimbledon House estate has abruptly ended just beyond the junction with Burghley Road. Below is a track leading to Somerset Road and the fields of the Dairy Farm which ten years later were to be bought by the All England Lawn Tennis Club. In the background is the line of Church Road, the grounds of Wimbledon Park Golf Club and in the distance the lake.

Now: The end of Marryat Road, June 1995, at the start of the Tennis Championships. An A.E.L.T.C. car drives away from the courts at the bottom of the road, while on the left a television cameraman on the end of the high gantry prepares to send pictures of the scene all over the world. Meanwhile, on the left at the corner of Burghley Road two modern houses have replaced the original mansion.

WIMBLEDON PARK LAKE AND GOLF COURSE.
Then: Wimbledon Park Lake and Golf Course from an unmade Home Park Road, about 1910. The land then still belonged to Lady Lane, daughter of John Augustus Beaumont who started the development of the Park in 1850. She had leased the land round the lake to a Golf Club, whose first club house is on the right. The lake had been created in the 1760s by Capability Brown for Earl Spencer; its boat house can be seen on the edge.

Now: Wimbledon Park Lake and Golf Course, 1995. The Council, owners of the Park since 1914, have recently sold the freehold of the golf course for over three million pounds to the All-England Club. But the future of the Golf Club is said to be assured. Its third club house on the right was built in the 1950s, after the first had been burnt down and the second destroyed by a bomb in the last war. Many of the original trees on the course survive (though not in this picture) and so, almost hidden in the background, does the lake.

ARTHUR ROAD.

Then: The bottom of Arthur Road with its unusual changes in width, about 1910. On the left is the Station Master's house and the entrance to the District Line Station, opened in 1889. Opposite are the offices of Ryan and Penfold, the estate agents who developed 'the Grid', the series of streets to the north of the road, between 1906 and 1914. In the background Arthur Road climbs towards the remains of the old Vineyard Hill Wood.

Now: Arthur Road today, with the trees in the foreground replacing those on the top of the hill. The original shops and houses mostly survive, but since this photograph was taken, Rashbrooks has become Hawes and Co. It is also interesting to see that the old changes in the width of the road have been used to help modern traffic calming measures.

THE END OF WORPLE ROAD.

Then: The end of Worple Road about 1910. Ladies alight from a tram going to Hammersmith, while a lady shielding herself from the sun talks to the driver of a second tram for Hampton Court. In the background on the left the original St. Mark's Church can just be seen. In the centre the Alexandra Hotel (named after Edward VII's Queen) is already over thirty years old, while J. and B. Marsh, Flour Merchants, had once owned Wimbledon Mill before Earl Spencer took it over in 1864.

Now: The end of Worple Road today. Both Elys and the Alexandra have been given radical face-lifts and have expanded in size (with the pub taking over J. and B. Marsh). But the shops along the pavement on the left are unchanged since they were cut in half in 1906 to make room for the double tram-track.

WORPLE ROAD FROM THE JUNCTION WITH RAYMOND ROAD

Then: Worple Road looking East from the junction with Raymond Road about 1910. The road here is only wide enough for a single tram track; it had to be broadened out to take two by Ely's corner, where a tram is turning into Hill Road. On the left are the gardens of large private houses, built in the late 1870s, and beyond them a sign advertising the Skating Rink in the Worple Arcade. Opposite is the Congregational church, completed in 1883, with its conspicuous spire.

Now: Worple Road from the new roundabout by Raymond Road, 1995. The picture well illustrates the transformation that has taken place in parts of the Town Centre since the 1970s. The Victorian houses and Congregational church (which was destroyed by a bomb) have been replaced by the massive British Telecom building on the left and the spikey General, Municipal and Boilermakers Union Headquarters opposite. And the road is now double the width – a far cry from the years before 1870 when it was a small cart track leading to the fields.

WORPLE ROAD FROM THE JUNCTION WITH MALCOLM ROAD.

Then: Worple Road looking west from the junction with Malcolm Road, 1915. A misty November day during the First World War with an officer walking by a large open space, with as yet no houses before St. George's College at the bottom of Ridgway Place. In the foreground is the entrance to Dr. Winton's surgery. In the background is a tram and the spire of the Methodist church.

Now: Worple Road from the junction with Malcolm Road today. Houses (mainly from the 1920s) and trees now fill the open space, while the surgery has become a hotel and the College has vanished. But the curb stones for the garage entrance in the foreground are still there and the stone setts are probably hidden under the tarmac.

NURSERY ROAD.
Then: Nursery Road and the entrance to the All-England Lawn Tennis Championships, June 1912. The latest taxis (with their spare wheels very evident) have brought spectators from the station, supervised by a solitary policeman. Just visible behind the stack of chairs on the right is a corner of the old Centre Court, and behind it are trees shielding the courts from the railway.

Now: Nursery Road, 1995, important today as the headquarters of the local Ambulance Service. The All-England Club gave up the grounds in 1921. They are now used by the girls of Wimbledon High School. Ornamental gates at the entrance commemorate the original site of the Tennis Championships, while at least one of the original Club buildings survives at their side – as do the trees in the background.

STATION APPROACH, RAYNES PARK.

Then: Station Approach, Raynes Park, about 1910. The London and South-Western Railway Station, which had opened in 1871, is hidden behind the railway cottages on the left, while the main line is hidden by high trees. Opposite is the Raynes Park Hotel, opened shortly after the Station, but recently rebuilt. The large building to its left was originally four private houses, but was converted in the 1880s into shops – a dairy, baker, tobacconist and grocer. Beyond is the distinguished-looking London and South-Western Bank, but then only three small shops before the corner of Amity Grove.

Now: Station Approach, Raynes Park, 1995. The station is now hidden behind parked cars, while the railway lines are still hidden – behind large advertisement hoardings as well as trees. The Raynes Park Hotel has expanded over its forecourt, as have the shops. The Bank is now a branch of Barclays, while beyond it an extra block of shops was added in the 1920s.

RAYNES PARK STATION.

Then: Raynes Park Station, about 1910. On the right is the entrance to the booking office and to the brick tunnel below the lines, built in 1838 to allow Edward Rayne to get his sheep to Kingston market. Beyond the Estate Office are two railway cottages (built in 1862 for signalmen after the Queen's Doctor had been killed in a serious accident here the previous year) – and the offices of 'coal merchants' who did good business in the area. In the background a train goes off to Waterloo, while a tram approaches from Wimbledon.

Now: Raynes Park Station today. The station buildings were modernised in 1935, with a bridge now linking the platforms. But the tunnel remains – for pedestrians and pigeons. The parade of shops replaced the old cottages and coal offices in the 1930s. The area is normally clogged with traffic whose flow is not helped by several pedestrian crossings and the special cycle-track.

RAYNES PARK STATION PLATFORM.
Then: Raynes Park Station Platform, about 1910. A South-Western local steam-train on the line to Dorking pulls in to the station. To the right is the Station-Master's house, to the left a high signal gantry.

Now: Raynes Park Station Platform, 1995. A Southern region electric train pulls in, as they have done ever since 1915 when the lines were at last electrified. But trees now hide both the old station-master's house (still there, but put to other uses) and the signals – now lights.

DURHAM ROAD.
Then: Durham Road about 1905. On the left are two parades of shops (originally known as Market Place and Commercial Place), built in the 1880s as part of the Amity estate development. In the background on the right is the temporary iron Anglican church, put up in the 1890s at the corner of Richmond Road. The site of the future St. Matthew's is in the foreground. In between is farm-land — with one of the chickens pecking away in the middle of the road.

Now: Durham Road today, like most roads in Wimbledon as much a parking-lot as a thoroughfare. On the right the second St. Matthew's church dominates the near-by houses (its predecessor was destroyed by a flying bomb in 1944). On the left the old shops are also dominated by modern buildings, but all have survived.

COOMBE LANE.

Then: Coombe Lane just to the east of the junction with West Barnes Lane, about 1912. A cart belonging to P. Bell and Sons, carmen of Garfield Road, South Wimbledon, proceeds slowly along a still very countrified Coombe Lane. Beyond it are the last remains of Haynts Wood which had covered this area for centuries. In the background is the last house in Durham Road, Kingsley Girls' School.

Now: Coombe Lane near the junction with West Barnes Lane in 1995, its one link with the past the back of the old school (now flats) in Durham Road. Cottenham Parade, built in the 1930s and till recently used only for shops, has now become a very popular place for eating-out. Far less popular is Merton Council's very controversial and very expensive cycle-track. Constructed in 1994, it has infuriated many residents in Coombe Lane, most local shop-keepers and all drivers – and is still not used by all cyclists. It is a fitting monument to Wimbledon's 'shot-gun marriage' to Merton, Mitcham and Morden thirty years ago.

BIOGRAPHIES

RICHARD MILWARD has lived in Wimbledon almost all his life. After gaining a history degree at Oxford, he taught at his old school, Wimbledon College, for forty years. Since retiring in 1985, he has devoted himself to local history and has written several books, the latest a very successful *Pictorial History*.

ROGER MUSGRAVE, a Wimbledon resident from 1959, has specialised in topographical and architectural photography since retiring from a career in advertising. His work has been published in *House and Garden* and in a scholarly study of the Romanesque sculptures of Canterbury Cathedral; and he has recorded important local buildings for the Wimbledon Society.

His pictures for this book were taken on Ilford FP4-Plus, 125 ASA black and white film, using a Pentax SP500 camera with Tamron 28-70mm, 3.5 zoom lens.

ANGELA RATHBONE has lived in Wimbledon for nearly fifty years. Her interests include Romanesque architecture, especially French, and travelling as widely and often as possible.

Her camera is a Minolta with a zoom lens 35-70 mm, f4. She used an Ilford HP5 black and white film.

NOTE ON THE 'NOW' PICTURES

The aim throughout has been to find the closest equivalent to the original views, differing only to avoid risk to life and limb (Edwardian photographers seemed to enjoy placing their cameras well into the roadway) or to emphasise what has changed (or not) in our selected locations during the past ninety-odd years. Our thanks to all the local citizens who positioned themselves and their vehicles, prams, bicycles, horses etc. so suitably for our visual compositions; to the Conservators of Wimbledon Common for readily granting permission for photography on their land; and not least to our local police and traffic wardens, whose forbearance enabled us to take all 44 views without incurring a single parking ticket or summons for obstruction.

Roger Musgrave.